EASTER VIBES

SADIE WORD

GREETINGS QUESTION SEEKERS!

Have you ever wanted to ride on the back of an Iguanodon dinosaur?

OR

Perhaps, you have been searching for a way to ask thought provoking questions to other humans for sport?

Well, this book can't help you with the Iguanodon until they come back from extinction, but it can help you start an engaging chat with other lifeforms!

This book is meant to inspire meaningful conversations with friends and family through oodles of thought provoking questions. Inspire loads of friendly inquiry with over 400 questions, enigmas, and conundrums!

So without any further ado, let the games begin!

DIRECTIONS:

Choose a reader.

Make sure to read the phrase, "Would you Rather-"
at the beginning of each question.

The reader will read the first question and everyone
will choose one of the choices given out loud.

Picking both or neither is not an option!

For the people who picked the least popular choice,
ask them why they chose that?

You can also write the answers down on mini
white boards, or make it into a points game!

PRO TIP:
Honestly, you really don't need to follow these directions.
They have been included for those who like to follow the rules
and need some boundaries. For all rule breaking rebels, please
disregard these direction pages and let pandemonium ensue!

Have jelly beans for teeth
OR
Have marshmallow fluff for hair?

Covered in feathers like a bird
OR
Covered in wool like a lamb?

Eat a whole bunch of carrots
OR
Drink a full glass of carrot juice?

Have your Easter basket be a rain boot
OR
Have your Easter basket be a tiny
flower pot?

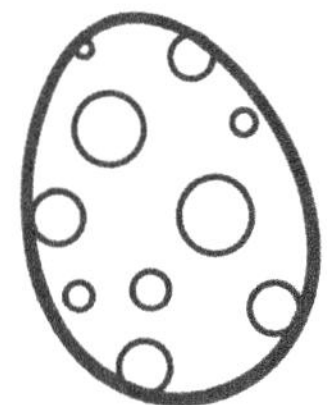

Spend the day playing with 20 baby chicks
OR
Spend the day playing with 20 baby
bunnies?

Plant a whole garden of flowers
OR
Plant an entire garden of vegetables?

Have your ears replaced with bunny ears
OR
Have your nose and mouth replaced
with a chicken beak?

Build a lemonade stand and sell your
homemade lemonade
OR
Get rid of things in your house and sell
them in a garage sale?

Have a talking pink rabbit for a pet
OR
Have a giant frog that is big enough to
carry you places as a pet?

Design and plant your own fairy garden
OR
Turn your backyard into a giant
field of wildflowers?

Be able to control when it rains
OR
Be able to control the temperature outside?

Become a caterpillar so that one day
you will become a butterfly
OR
Become a tadpole so that one day
you will become a frog?

Attend a tea party by the Mad Hatter
OR
Play a game of croquet with the
Queen of Hearts?

Make your own Easter candy ice cream
OR
Make your own Masterpiece in
chalk on the driveway?

Live on Easter Island (Chile) for the
rest of your life
OR
Live on Christmas Island (Australia)
for the rest of your life?

Would you Rather?

Be best friends with the Easter Bunny
OR
Be best friends with Santa Claus?

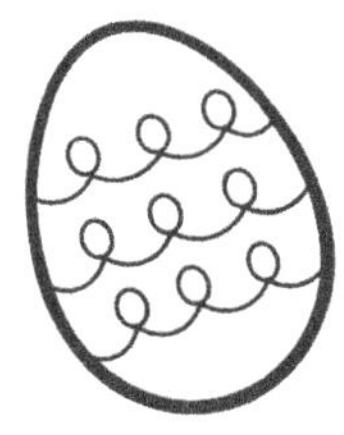

Sing like a songbird
OR
Jump like a frog?

Be completely covered in ladybugs
for a day
OR
Be followed by 100 toads that
jumped on you all day?

Decorate 100 Easter eggs
OR
Find 100 Easter eggs?

Find a pot of gold coins at the end
of a rainbow
OR
Find a lifetime supply of chocolate
coins at the end of a rainbow?

Pick berries fresh out of your own
garden every morning
OR
Cut flowers to make a bouquet from
your own garden every day?

Have another sibling
OR
Adopt a new pet?

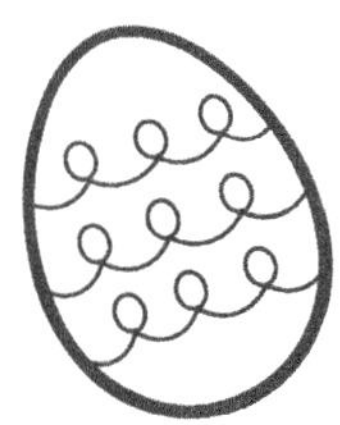

Live in a giant bird's nest up in the trees
OR
Live in a rabbit hole in the ground?

Jump into a swimming pool full of
Marshmallows
OR
Bathe in Hot Cocoa?

Decorate Easter eggs with galaxy swirls
OR
Decorate Easter eggs with golden
temporary tattoos?

Have it be Springtime all year round
OR
Have it be Autumn all year round?

Have giant butterfly wings on your back
that allow you to fly
OR
Have the ability to make any plant grow
with one touch from your green thumb?

 Would you Rather?

Lose your sense of taste
OR
Lose your sense of smell?

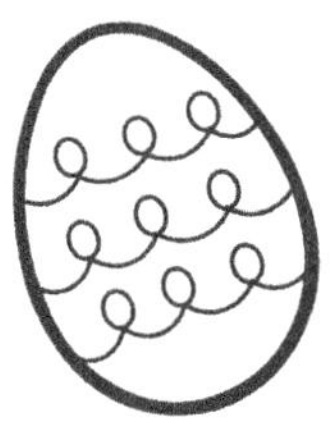

Wear a fancy Easter bonnet for
an entire month
OR
Wear pink bunny ears for a whole month?

Play frisbee like a dog and catch
it in your mouth
OR
Play soccer like a dog and move the ball
with your nose?

Kiss a frog to grant you one wish
OR
Catch a leprechaun to make you rich?

Have to jump rope for a whole day
OR
Hula hoop for an entire day?

Eat mystery flavored Jelly Beans
OR
Eat mystery flavored Marshmallows?

Would you Rather?

Decorate Easter eggs like your
favorite book characters
OR
Decorate Easter eggs like your
favorite animals?

Be given one million peeps
OR
Be given one million creme filled eggs?

Live in a sandy desert
OR
Live in a frozen wasteland?

Paint your Easter eggs to
look like avocados
OR
Make feet for your eggs and make it
look like a chicken is hatching?

Have hair the color of carrots
OR
Have carrot leaves for hair?

Have a hummingbird perch on your finger
OR
Have a bluebird visit you every morning at
your window as you wake up?

Spend a whole day decorating a dozen
Easter eggs
OR
Spend two hours decorating just
one Easter egg?

Be followed by rainbows wherever you go
OR
Have flowers bloom under your feet
wherever you go?

See the world in only neon colors
OR
See the world in only pastel colors?

Make a bird feeder
OR
Make a birdhouse?

Hang prisms around your room to cast
rainbows everywhere
OR
Decorate your room with
glow-in-the-dark constellations?

Plant a butterfly bush
OR
Plant red flowers to attract hummingbirds?

Make S'mores with Peeps
OR
Make Bunny Butt cupcakes?

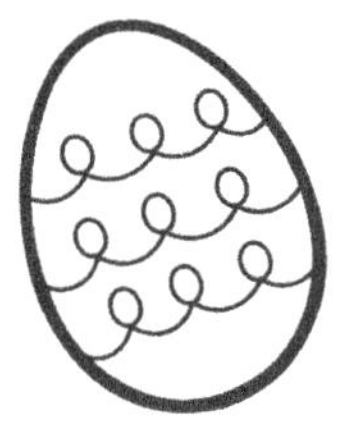

Eat a chocolate bunny filled
with peanut butter
OR
Eat a chocolate bunny filled with caramel?

Have rainbows for eyebrows
OR
Have a cottontail like a bunny?

Become a lamb for a day
OR
Become a lion for a year?

Wear a giant Easter hat made of candy
OR
Wear a suit made of plastic Easter eggs?

Have an Easter egg filled with a fortune
cookie fortunes that come true
OR
Have an Easter egg filled with magic beans
from Jack and the Beanstalk?

Eat a ham dinner for Easter
OR
Eat a lamb dinner for Easter?

Go around a whole week dressed
in an Easter bunny costume
OR
Go around a whole week dressed as a
chick hatching from an Easter egg?

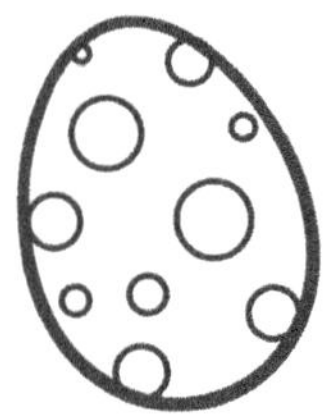

Live in a world with rainbow-colored rain
that splashes the world with color
OR
Live in a world where flowers
can talk to you?

Ride a llama wearing pink bunny ears
that spits chocolate
OR
Drive a car that looks like an Easter basket?

Go without the internet and
electricity on Easter Day
OR
Go without getting any baskets or
candy for Easter?

Own a chicken that lays one
golden egg a year
OR
Own a rabbit that lays 1 dozen
chocolate eggs a day?

Have flowers growing out of your head
OR
Have butterflies flying out of your ears?

Have every day include an Easter egg hunt
OR
Have every day include a basket of goodies
you find at the end of the day?

Have a whole month of down-pouring rain
OR
Live on the Mayflower ship for a whole
month at sea?

Would you Rather?

Have the job of making chocolate rabbits
OR
Have the task of designing Easter bonnets?

Have the chance to meet your hero and
spend a whole day with them
OR
Get the chance to meet a mythical creature
and spend a week with them?

Be required to find 35 items on a daily
scavenger hunt
OR
Never have to participate in a scavenger
hunt or Easter egg hunt again?

Directions:

The oldest person in the room gets to read first.

Make sure to read the phrase, "Who would be the most likely to-" at the beginning of each question.

Read a question and have everyone (including the reader) point at the person in the room that best fits the statement.

The person who has the most people pointing at them gets the point and also gets to read the next question.

Continue this until someone gets 10 points or (if you're having too much fun) you run out of questions!

To find a whole field of four-leaf clovers?

Make the most spectacular Easter wreath?

To have an umbrella that looks like a giant duck face?

Win the first Corn Hole
game of the year?

Have a baby chick follow them home?

Make a life-size fairy garden?

Drink a milkshake out of a hollow
chocolate bunny?

Find their Easter basket first?

Decorate a tree with colorful
Easter eggs?

Have a garden filled with gnomes?

Go singing in the rain?

Eat a carrot like Bugs Bunny?

Spring clean the entire house on their own?

Have rain boots that have funny designs?

Find an Easter Island statue that looks like them?

Dance in the rain?

Go swing on a swing at the park as soon as it's nice out?

Send someone snail mail?

Go to a baseball game?

Make homemade ice cream?

Wear flowers in their hair?

Go to a car wash?

Plant new flowers in the spring?

Visit a museum?

Read outside?

Unplug for 24 hours?

Go camping in the backyard?

Try a new recipe for Easter?

Go on a bike ride?

Plan a trip to a National Park?

Go birdwatching?

Paint in rainbow colors?

Go to garage sales?

Make an origami bunny?

Start and finish a puzzle?

Participate in a watermelon eating contest?

Wear bunny ears for the entire month of April?

Bake an Easter-themed cake?

Spend a day at the zoo?

Go horseback riding through
a nature trail?

Make their own scavenger hunt?

Sleep under the stars?

Make a wish by blowing on
dandelion seeds?

Hop around the house like a bunny?

Visit a cathedral?

Never miss a Sunday Mass?

Not afraid to get dirty while gardening?

Twirl around in a vast field of flowers?

Go hiking in the mountains?

Find the end of a rainbow?

Find every egg without a sweat?

Directions:

There are some crazy jelly bean flavors out there!
In this game you must choose which flavors you
would want to eat as fast as you can.

Pick a reader and pick one other person to
answer as many questions as they
can in under 30 seconds.

You must pick one Jelly Bean flavor that you
would prefer to snack on. You cannot answer
both or neither, you must choose one!

Your score is determined by the number
of questions, you answer.
Example: If you answer 7 questions in 30 seconds,
your score will be 7.

Give everyone a turn to answer as many questions as
they can. Whoever has the most points wins!

If there is a tie, see how many questions
can be answered in 15 seconds.

Whoever answers the most questions in
the tiebreaker wins!

Carrots OR Strawberry Rhubarb?

Orange Popsicle OR Boston Creme?

Malt Ball OR Deviled Eggs?

Hazelnut OR Key Lime?

Bubble gum OR Buttered popcorn?

Chocolate pudding OR Orange Sherbet?

Toothpaste OR Dishsoap?

Lemon Lime OR Sour Cherry?

Grass OR Dirt?

Peach OR Strawberry-banana?

Pomegranate OR Kiwi?

Mixed Berry Smoothie OR Root Beer?

Booger OR Vomit?

Pink Lemonade OR White Chocolate?

Dog Food OR Spoiled Milk?

Pear OR Coconut?

Fluffernutter OR Lemon Poppy?

Beets OR Goat Cheese?

Green Apple OR Cinnamon?

Watermelon OR Toasted Marshmallow?

Pineapple OR French Vanilla?

Stink Bug OR Mud Pie?

Boston Creme OR Peanut Butter?

Butter Pecan OR Cake Batter?

Coffee OR Rocky Road?

Almond OR Toffee?

Fudge OR Pumpkin Spice?

Lavender OR Blueberry?

Turmeric OR Curry?

Fruit Punch OR Grape?

Peppermint OR Ginger?

Stinky Socks OR Farts?

S'mores OR Cannoli?

Cookie dough OR Salted Caramel?

Lamb chops OR Spring Peas?

Pistachio OR Blackberry?

Birthday Cake OR Cotton Candy?

Honey Ham OR Gravy?

Green Tea OR Cookies & Cream?

Red Velvet OR Walnut?

Corn on the Cob OR Buttermilk Pancakes?

Blue Cheese OR Lobster?

Fruit Cake OR Chai Latte?

Black Pepper OR Nutmeg?

Prune OR Asparagus?

Hot Sauce OR Maple Syrup?

Cactus Water OR Oat Milk?

Bacon OR Corndog?

Irish Creme OR Chocolate Orange?

Espresso OR Buttercream?

Mocha OR Butterscotch?

Honey OR Chili Pepper?

Directions:

Let the shortest person start as the reader.

The reader will ask the person to their left
the question, "Truth or Dare"?

The person who is asked "Truth or Dare" will decide
whether they want to answer a Truth Question or
perform a Dare. You cannot change your mind after
choosing Truth or Dare.

All Truth questions will be found on the left pages.
AND
All Dares will be found on the right pages.

When that person has completed their Truth or Dare,
the reader will then pass the book to the person
on their right.

Warning!

You cannot lie when you choose a Truth question.
AND
No matter what the dare is, you have to do it.

The Truth questions are designed to have everyone
share something little known about themselves.
AND
The Dares are designed to challenge the person
attempting them, not to embarrass them.

If needed: Set a time limit for how long a person has
to complete the Truth or Dare.

What do you think is the
worst Easter candy?

Are you scared of any bugs?

What is your favorite Easter tradition?

Eat a carrot like a bunny

Be overly egg-cited about everything
for the next two turns

Text someone, "Happy Easter!" Only
using your nose

What is your favorite vegetable
to eat uncooked?

If you had your own business, what
would it be?

Name three things that make you feel
#blessed

For the next two turns, stick out your front teeth like a bunny

Hop around the entire room like a bunny for a minute

Sing the Peter Cottontail song while someone makes bunny ears behind you

If you had a pet dinosaur, which
would you pick?

If you had a time machine, who would
you visit in the past or future
on Easter Day?

Which Harry Potter magical creature
do you wish was real?

Try moving your ears without
touching them

Show the room your silliest Bunny Hop
dance moves

Try to touch your nose with your
tongue

What is your favorite jelly bean flavor?

What is the funniest word or phrase
you can think of?

Have you ever fed a carrot to a dog?

Make baby chick noises until your next turn

Burrow under blankets and pillows for two turns, then jump out and announce, "It's SPRING!"

Find yourself a fluffy bunny tail and shake that cottontail with a funny dance

If you could only listen to one song for the rest of your life, what would it be?

Have you ever licked a plate clean before?

What is the worst Easter candy you have ever tried?

Roar like a lion as loud as you can

Pretend you are constantly
finding very sticky Easter eggs
until your next turn

Go outside and yell, "Happy Easter,
everyone!" At the top of your lungs

What is the creepiest animal?

What kind of famous person would you like to be and why?

Have you ever gotten a stomach ache from overeating your Easter candy?

For the next three turns, randomly ask everyone, "What's up, Doc?"

Prank call a friend or family member who isn't with you now

Build a nest with things around you like a bird and sit in it for two turns

What is your favorite book?

Could you go for 5 days without food or 5 days without using any technology?

Would you go to school wearing a full Easter bunny costume for $50.00?

Walk and cluck like a chicken
for one turn

Take a silly Easter selfie with everyone
in the room

Crack an Easter egg over your head

If you were any farm animal,
which would you be?

What would you like to find at
the end of a rainbow?

Have you ever seen anyone
faint in front of you?

Pick a person in the room and tell them why you are grateful for them

Pretend to be a T-Rex trying to pick up an Easter egg it found

Skip around the room until your next turn

Have you ever eaten someone else's
Easter candy?

What is the silliest fear you have?

If you could change any house rules,
what would they be?

Pretend you are at a tea party and keep sipping imaginary tea for a whole turn, remember to keep that pinky up!

Have someone blindfold you and feed you one piece of Easter candy. Try and guess what it is!

Go outside and hug something in your yard for one whole minute

What Easter tradition would you like
to add or change to how your family
celebrates the holiday?

What is your favorite thing to order at
a cafe or coffee shop?

Have you ever kept a plant alive longer
than one year?

Juggle plastic eggs

Wear Easter basket grass on your
head for the next two turns and
keep asking people around you,
"Do you like my hat?"

Make an Easter-themed outfit and strut
your stuff on a carpet (your runway)

If your hair could be any crazy color, what would you change it to?

If you had a space ship, what would you name it?

What is your favorite springtime smell?

Stand outside with a sign that says:
"Honk if you can read"

Sing "Mary had a Little Lamb" while
hopping on one foot

Go outside and pose like a gnome in
your garden and have someone take a
picture and send it with no context to
three people

Directions:

Let the person with the longest hair,
read the first page of questions.

Make sure to read the phrase, "Never have I ever-"
at the beginning of each question.

Anyone who can answer "yes, I have done this
thing you speak of" to a question gets a point.

The first person to get to 15 points wins!

Other fun ways to play:
Snacking Game - Everyone is given 10 to 20 sweets.
Whoever runs out of sweets first, wins!
Pro tip:
This version is best played with small
snacks like popcorn, jelly beans, M&Ms, etc.

And for those who have already snacked:

Ten Fingers Game - Everyone holds up all ten fingers.
If you can say "yes" to any of these statements,
you put down one finger. The first one
to put down all their fingers wins!

Seen a double rainbow?

Made cinnamon buns with bunny ears?

Flown a kite?

Had a piece of Carrot cake?

Blown bubbles bigger than my head?

Went sky gazing to find shapes and
animals in the clouds?

Decorated Easter cookies?

Seen the Cherry Blossoms in
Washington, D.C.?

Had a picnic outside?

Played baseball or softball?

Eaten all my Easter candy in one week?

Gone horseback riding?

Gone barefoot for a whole day?

Made pastel-colored macaroons?

Grown a vegetable?

Decorated eggs to look like
tiny cactus plants?

Twirled on a lamppost and sung
"Singing in the Rain"?

Gone to a farm to go berry picking?

Won a game of mini-golf?

Worn a fancy outfit on Easter?

Found a four-leaf clover?

Had a ladybug land on me?

Needed help finding my Easter basket?

Caught a butterfly?

Seen the end of a rainbow?

Attended an egg race?

Had a bonfire in spring?

Splashed in puddles on a rainy day?

Held or seen an ostrich egg?

Went to an outdoor sports game?

Hosted a tea party?

Seen an Easter Parade?

Decorated over two dozen Easter
eggs in one sitting?

Painted rocks with fun designs?

Made my own walking stick out of
a fallen branch for a hike?

Blown on a blade of grass between my
fingers to make it whistle?

Gone on a 100 mile road trip?

Decorated a real hollowed chicken egg?

Planted flowers for the bees?

Gone camping in one of the
National Parks?

Covered a whole driveway or
sidewalk in chalk art?

Seen a sunrise?

Visited the mall Easter bunny?

Worn Easter bunny ears in public?

Climbed a tree?

Fed ducks at a pond?

Gone somewhere tropical for
Spring Break?

Made a flower crown to wear?

Played Bean Boozled?

Made rainbow colored cupcakes?

Gone strawberry picking?

Snuggled up under a blanket and read a
book on a rainy day?

Listened to the bumblebees hum in a garden?

Learned the names and calls of my backyard birds?

Let in the fresh air on the first warm day of the year?

Held a bunny?

Bought a funny umbrella?

Tried the gross jelly beans from
Harry Potter?

Skipped rocks on a lake?

Watch birds build a nest and watch their
babies hatch?

Read a book outside?

Slept with the windows open?

Taken a nap in a hammock?

Had a ride on a tractor?

Camped out in the backyard waiting
for the Easter Bunny to arrive?

Watched a sunset?

Picked a bunch of wildflowers to
make a bouquet?

Rolled down a grassy hill?

THANK YOU!

You are the most marvelous person for
purchasing this book, thank you!

Congratulations on adopting this charming
little edition into your home library! If it has
brought you even a thimble full of joy,
please consider leaving a review for it
on Amazon.com

I shall wait patiently for your comments,
my dear readers. Any guidance you are
willing to bestow unto me helps me take
another step closer to becoming
the Grand Poobah of Game Books.

Help the cause, start a trend, and write a review!

Also by Sadie Word:

Also by Nyx Spectrum:

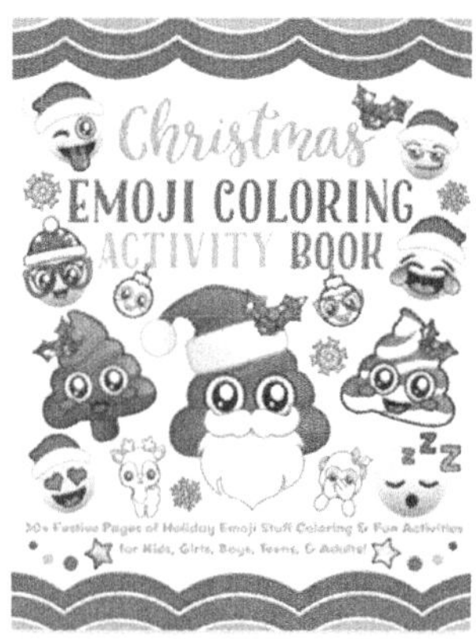

Made in the USA
Monee, IL
07 July 2026

56555724R00056